Goat on a Tractor

For Brian and Sandy

– Amy

For Beth and Kevin

– Ross

Goat on a Tractor

Amy Harrop

Illustrated by Ross Hamilton

BATEMAN BOOKS

Lily was moody, **Lily** was glum,
she had nothing to do, she was looking for fun.
The cows were off grazing, the pigs rolled in grass,
the rest of the farmyard were watching clouds pass.

She'd **swung** on the washing and **chewed** on some pears,
jumped on the tramp and **slid** down the stairs.
Lily wanted some action, to learn something new,
she longed for excitement, an adventure or two.

Down the back of the farm, parked in a shed,
was the farmer's old tractor, all rusty and red.

Lily began to hatch a new plot,
could she drive that old tractor? She'd give it a shot!

Lily waited until the coast was clear,

leapt on the tractor and put it in gear.

It rolled out of the barn with a **splutter** and **cough,**

then headed straight for the water trough!

In a panic,
Lily corrected her steering,
down past the shed,
where the farmer was shearing.

But as she attempted to put on the brake,
her hoof hit the accelerator by **mistake!**

The rusty old tractor suddenly lurched into action,
missing a fencepost by only a fraction,
it took off downhill, hitting a bump,
sending **Lily** airborne in a
stunt-worthy jump!

She cleared the first paddock with the greatest of ease,
flew straight through a cloud of bewildered bees,

jumped ten bales of hay, a creek and the mower
before the old tractor decided to lower.

The wheels hit the ground with a **rumble** and **thump**,
then were knocked to the side by some gorse in a clump.

The next thing she knew, the tractor had spun,
sending **Lily** downhill on a backwards run!

She reversed through a field of perplexed-looking sheep,

hooning down the paddock, long and steep,

a panicked **Lily** tried to slam on the brake,

because, coming up fast, there was the . . . lake!

With a **crash** and a **splash**, the tractor went in,
the animals came running at the sound of the din.
The tractor **bubbled**, then the engine **choked**,
Lily sat in the lake,
dripping
and
soaked.

'Look at your mess!' the animals cried.

'You've ruined the farm with your tractor joyride!

You've dug up the paddocks, knocked over the silage,

and broken the fences through your tractor mileage.'

Lily looked around at the damage she'd done.
She had upset her friends while having her fun,
Lily knew she had to make it right,
she would clean up the farm if it took her all night!

She lifted a hoof and made a vow,
'I will make it right, every way I know how.

But please, oh please help me out of this lake.
And as soon as I can, I will fix my **mistake**.'

The animals made a farmyard chain,

the horse and the cows taking most of the strain.

They **tugged** and they **heaved** to pull **Lily** free,

and rescued the tractor with the help of a tree.

Lily Goat was as good as her pledge,
she mended the railings and fixed up the hedge,
flattened the paddocks and settled the bees,
deciding it was time to hang up the keys . . .

. . . almost!

This edition published by David Bateman Ltd, 2025
Unit 2/5 Workspace Drive, Hobsonville,
Auckland 0618, New Zealand
www.batemanbooks.co.nz

ISBN: 978-1-77689-159-7

A catalogue record for this book is available
from the National Library of New Zealand.

Designed by Cheryl Smith
Printed in China by Toppan Leefong Printing Ltd